DINOSAUR DAYS
STEGOSAURUS

HEIGHT: 9′ (2.7 M)

HEIGHT: 5′ (1.5 M)

DINOSAUR DAYS
STEGOSAURUS

SARA GILBERT

CREATIVE EDUCATION CREATIVE PAPERBACKS

Table of Contents

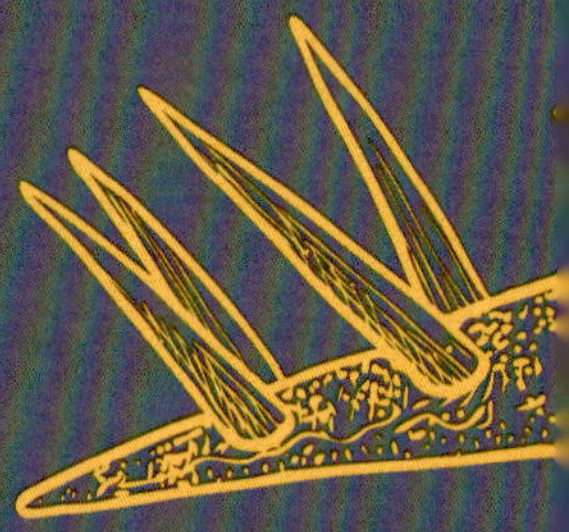

Published by Creative Education
and Creative Paperbacks
P.O. Box 227, Mankato,
Minnesota 56002
Creative Education and Creative
Paperbacks are imprints of
The Creative Company
www.thecreativecompany.us

Book design by Blue Design
(www.bluedes.com)
Art direction by Rita Marshall
Printed in the United States of America

Photographs by Alamy (tony
french, Imagery and Imagination),
Bridgeman Images (Arthur
Oxenham), Dover Clip Art, Getty
Images (DEA Picture Library),
Thinkstock (chronicler101,
CoreyFord, Dorling Kindersley,
dottedhippo, Gluiki, Jupiterimages,
leonello, Pimpay, rikkyal,
Vac1, Warpaintcobra)

Library of Congress Cataloging-in-Publication Data
Names: Gilbert, Sara, author.
Title: Stegosaurus / Sara Gilbert.
Series: Dinosaur days.
Includes bibliographical references and index.
Summary: This introductory exploration uncovers the discovery of *Stegosaurus* fossils before revealing information about its era, features, and lifestyle, as well as its eventual extinction.
Identifiers: ISBN 978-1-64026-049-8 (hardcover) / ISBN 978-1-62832-637-6 (pbk) / ISBN 978-1-64000-165-7 (eBook)

This title has been submitted for CIP processing under LCCN 2018938976.

CCSS: RI.1.1, 2, 4, 5, 6, 7; RI.2.1, 2, 5, 6, 7; RI.3.1, 2, 5, 7; RF.1.1, 3, 4; RF.2.3, 4

First Edition HC 9 8 7 6 5 4 3 2 1
First Edition PBK 9 8 7 6 5 4 3 2 1

SOUND-IT-OUT: *Stegosaurus:* *STEG-uh-SAWR-us*

Meet *Stegosaurus*!

Welcome to the Natural History Museum in London, England. Meet Sophie! She is the world's most complete *Stegosaurus* **skeleton**. She has been here since 2014.

Sophie was found at Red Canyon Ranch in Wyoming in 2003.

SOUND-IT-OUT: paleontologists: *pay-lee-on-TOL-o-gists*

Bone Wars

The first *Stegosaurus* bones were found in 1876 in Colorado. Many **fossils** were found at that time. **Paleontologists** often fought about the bones they found. *Stegosaurus* means "roofed lizard."

***STEGOSAURUS* GREW TO ABOUT 25 OR 30 FEET (7.6–9.1 M) IN LENGTH.**

Back to the Jurassic

Stegosaurus fossils have been found in North America and Europe. It lived during the late Jurassic period. *Apatosaurus* was around then, too.

SOUND-IT-OUT: Jurassic: *jeh-RAS-ick*

FOSSILS OF SMALLER *STEGOSAURUS* RELATIVES HAVE BEEN DUG UP ALL AROUND THE WORLD.

SOUND-IT-OUT:
Apatosaurus:
ah-PAT-uh-SAWR-us

EARLY ON, SCIENTISTS THOUGHT *STEGOSAURUS* PLATES LAY ALONG ITS BACK, LIKE FISH SCALES.

Spikes and Spines

This dinosaur was easy to spot. It had a row of flat plates called scutes. These stuck out of its back. Long spikes grew out of the end of its tail. *Stegosaurus* swung its tail to fight off **predators**.

Stegosaurus was large and heavy. Its tiny head did not have much room for a brain. Scientists think its brain may have been the size of a walnut!

Timeline

227 MILLION YEARS AGO
LATE TRIASSIC

205 MILLION YEARS AGO
EARLY JURASSIC

180 MILLION YEARS AGO
MID-JURASSIC

***STEGOSAURUS* LIVED HERE!**

159 MILLION YEARS AGO
LATE JURASSIC

144 MILLION YEARS AGO
EARLY CRETACEOUS

98 MILLION YEARS AGO
LATE CRETACEOUS

Slow and Steady

Stegosaurus ate plants. It probably snacked on plants close to the ground. Its short neck could not reach very far. It used its beaky nose to tear leaves. Small teeth chomped the food.

Its back legs were much longer than its front legs. This made *Stegosaurus* slow. It may have stood up on its back legs to reach higher branches.

Stegosaurus *may have lived in groups called herds.*

STEGOSAURUS **AND OTHER PLANT-EATING DINOSAURS LIVED PEACEFULLY AS NEIGHBORS.**

So Long, *Stegosaurus*

At the end of the Jurassic, *Stegosaurus* died out. No one knows why it became **extinct**. Scientists hope to find out more about what happened!

Glossary

extinct — having no living members

fossils — bones or plants preserved for millions of years

paleontologists — scientists who study fossils

predators — animals that hunt other animals for food

skeleton — the bones that support a body

Read More

Barrett, Paul M. *Stegosaurus: An Extraordinary Specimen and the Secrets It Reveals.* London: Natural History Museum, 2017.

Pimentel, Annette Bay. *Do You Really Want to Meet Stegosaurus?* North Mankato, Minn.: Amicus, 2018.

Index

Websites

DK Find Out!: Stegosaurus
https://www.dkfindout.com/us/dinosaurs-and-prehistoric-life/dinosaurs/stegosaurus/
See an image of *Stegosaurus*, and take a dinosaur quiz!

National Geographic Kids: Stegosaurus
https://kids.nationalgeographic.com/animals/stegosaurus/#stegosaurus-side.jpg
Learn more about *Stegosaurus* and other dinosaurs.